Acoustic Praise

Songs for the Growing Choir

3 The Earth is the Lord's

16 Come, Walk With Me

23 Train Up a Child

33 On Jordan's Stormy Banks

45 Hear Us, O Father

57 I Will Rejoice and Be Glad

67 Lord of Life

75 One Day We'll Stand

87 A Choral Benediction

*Instrumental parts for each song can be found on the Instrumental Pack (CD-ROM) – 35028712

GlorySound

A DIVISION OF SHAWNEE PRESS, INC.

EXCLUSIVELY DISTRIBUTED BY HAL LEONARD CORPORATION

Visit Shawnee Press Online at
www.shawneepress.com

FOREWORD

This helpful choral songbook contains classic and newly composed songs arranged with sensitivity to smaller and developing choirs. Special care was taken to include worship resources that sound rich and full, even in SAB formats.

The acoustic qualities of the arrangements are a special feature to this collection. Each song has an optional instrumental obbligato, and most songs have optional acoustic guitar and bass charts. All of these options can be found on the Instrumental Pack CD-ROM. Should you not have instrumentalists to perform these parts, a folk-like StudioTrax CD is also available.

It is our prayer that this collection will bring glory to God and that it will be a useful tool as you minister to your community of faith.

- The Publisher

THE EARTH IS THE LORD'S

for S.A.B. voices, accompanied,
with optional flute (or C-instrument)

Words by WES HANNIBAL (ASCAP)

Music by
DIANE HANNIBAL (ASCAP)
Arranged by
ROGER THORNHILL (BMI)

4

all that is in it. He made the land and the sea. The

heav - ens de - clare, the stars sing His glo - ry.

Stones shout His prais - es in great sym - pho - ny.

Al - le - lu - ia, sing of His won - ders. Al - le - lu - ia, let

earth lift its voice! Al - le - lu - ia, sing of His splen - dor.

Let ev - 'ry nation and all of cre - a - tion re - joice!

Lift a ju - bi - lant noise!

The earth is the Lord's and
all that is in it. He made the moun-tains and plains, the

ALL VOICES UNISON

all of cre-a-tion re-joice! Lift a ju-bi-lant noise!

*For_____ the__

beau — ty of the earth, for the

* Tune: DIX, by Conrad Kocher (1786-1872); Words by Folliott S. Pierpont (1835-1917).

glo - ry of the skies.

For_____ the_

For_____ the_

love which from our birth o - ver

and a - round us lies.

Lord of all, to You we raise

this our hymn of grate - ful praise.

Al - le - lu - ia, sing of His won - ders. Al - le - lu - ia, let

14

earth lift it's voice! Al - le - lu - ia, sing of His splen-dor.

Let ev - 'ry na - tion and all of cre - a - tion re - joice!

COME, WALK WITH ME

for S.A.B. voices, accompanied,
with optional flute (or C-instrument)

Words by
JOSEPH M. MARTIN (BMI)

Music by
JAMES M. STEVENS (ASCAP)

trails of Gal - i - lee where Je - sus walked His earth - ly

days. Come, walk with me; come, walk with me.

mf

Come, walk with

18

20

TRAIN UP A CHILD

for S.A.B. voices, accompanied,
with optional flute (or C-instrument)

Inspired by Proverbs 22:6

Words and Music by
PEPPER CHOPLIN (ASCAP)

truth, guide the way, teach them prom-is-es God_ has made, that they may live in God's love and grace.

28

Train up a child; your re-wards will go be-yond_____ the days_ you live._ Raise them in love;_ gen-er-a-tions will be

30

ON JORDAN'S STORMY BANKS

for S.A.B. voices, accompanied,
with optional violin (or C-instrument)

Words by
SAMUEL STENNETT (1727-1795)

Music by
MATT LIMBAUGH (ASCAP)

34

Ca - naan's fair__ and__ hap - py land, where__ my pos - ses - sions

lie.   I am

one e-ter-nal day. There God, the Son, for-

ev-er reigns and scat-ters night a-way. No

bound for the prom - ised land,_____ I am bound for the prom - ised

land._____ O__ who will come__ and__ go with me? I am

bound for the prom - ised land. O____ who will
come___ and___ go with___ me? I am

44

HEAR US, O FATHER

for S.A.B. voices, accompanied,
with optional flute (or C-instrument)

Words by DON BESIG
and NANCY PRICE (ASCAP)

Music by
DON BESIG (ASCAP)

faith seems hard to find._____

Help us, O Fa - ther to know_____

Help us, O Fa - ther to

* Tune: TRENTHAM by Robert Jackson (1842-1914); Words by Edwin Hatch (1835-1889), alt..

fill us with life a - new._____

That__ we__ may__ love the__ things You__ love, and

do____ what____ You would do._____

Walk with us Fa - ther, each day.

Teach us to serve and o - bey. Give us the

strength_____ to be-lieve_____ You will sup-ply our ev-'ry need._____

strength, the strength to be-lieve_____

Lyrics under the staves:
strong,_____ stead - fast and true. Fa - ther we
give our lives_____ to

for the Ageless Wonders, Lynchburg, VA
Co-directors: Frances Howard and Erma Styles

I WILL REJOICE AND BE GLAD

for S.A.B. voices, accompanied,
with optional flute (or C-instrument)

Based on
PSALM 118:24

Words and Music by
JOSEPH M. MARTIN (BMI)

I will re-joice_ and be glad. This is the day_ that the

Lord hath made. I will re-joice,_ lift up my voice._

I will re-joice_ and be glad.

I will re-joice,_ lift up my voice._ I will re-joice_ and be

glad. I will re-

won - drous love._____ I will pro - claim His truth to

I will de - clare His truth.

all the world, and praise Him

lift up my voice,___ I will re-joice___ and be glad.

I will re-joice and be glad.___

LORD OF LIFE

for S.A.B. voices, accompanied,
with optional C or B♭ instrument

Words by
J. PAUL WILLIAMS (ASCAP)

Music by
JAMES M. STEVENS (ASCAP)

68

give my all to You. Lord, I know Your love will see me through.

give my all to You. Lord, Your love will see me through.

Lead me, Lord, in ev - 'ry-thing I do. Lord of Life,

(optional)

I give my all to You.

Lord of Life, I need Your cleans - ing pow'r. Lord, I need Your

pres-ence ev-'ry hour. Lord of Life, lead me, Lord. Lord of

Lord of Life, there is none like You.

Life, Lord of Life, I give my all to You.

great - ly to be___ praised.___ Lord of Life, I

give my all to You. Lord, I know Your love will see me through.

I give my all to You.

ONE DAY WE'LL STAND

for S.A.B. voices, accompanied,
with optional flute (or C-instrument)

Words and Music by
JON PAIGE (BMI)

songs of grief_ we'll then for - get, re - placed_ by joy - ful

sound, re - placed_ by joy - ful sound.

al - le - lu - ias   to   the   Lamb   for   all   e - ter - ni -

unis.

ty.

mp   cresc. poco a poco

(Play) cresc. poco a poco

* Words by John P. Rees (1828-1900).

sun, we've no less days__ to sing God's praise than

when__ we first be - gun, than when__ we first be -

rit.

song shall ev - er be,_____ great al - le - lu - ias

to the Lamb for all e - ter - ni - ty, great

A CHORAL BENEDICTION

for S.A.B. voices, accompanied,
with optional flute (or C-instrument)

Words by DON BESIG
and NANCY PRICE (ASCAP)

Music by
DON BESIG (ASCAP)

day._____ May the light of God shine on us to-day._

May it show us where to trav - el, lead us

back if we_ should stray.____ May the light of God

shine on us to-day.

May the love of God live in us to-day.

90

all we do and say. May the love of God

live in us to-day. May the peace of God

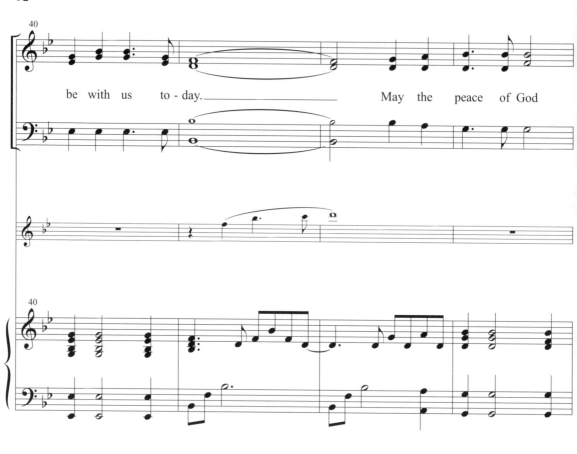

be with us to-day._____ May the peace of God

be with us to-day._____ May it guide us and pro-

tect us as we go our sep - 'rate ways._____ May the

peace of God be with us,

May the love of God

94